Spanish-English Picture Dictionary

First published in Great Britain in 2004 by Brimax™.
A division of Autumn Publishing Limited
Appledram Barns, Chichester PO20 7EQ

Text © 2004 Autumn Publishing Limited
Illustrations by Adam Pescott
Spanish language consultant Eleanor Hughes

Printed in 2004. This edition published in 2004 by Waterbird Books,
an imprint of School Specialty Children's Publishing, a member of the School Specialty Family.

Send all inquiries to:
School Speciality Children's Publishing
8720 Orion Place
Columbus, Ohio 43240-2111

www.ChildrensSpecialty.com

Library of Congress Cataloging-in-Publication Data is on file with the publisher.

0-7696-3526-1

Printed in China.

1 2 3 4 5 6 7 8 9 10 BRI 09 08 07 06 05 04

Contents

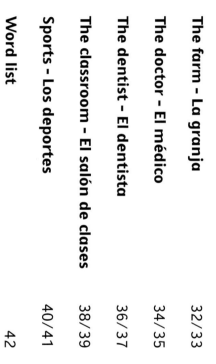
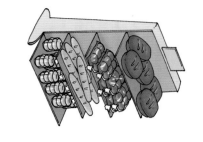
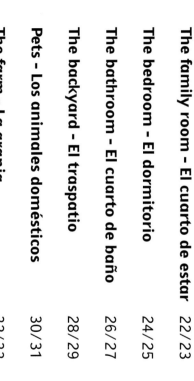

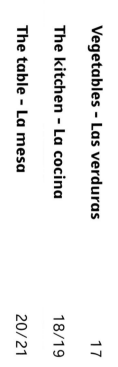
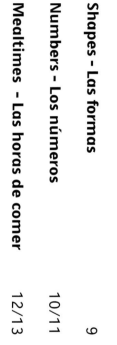
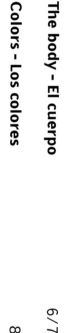
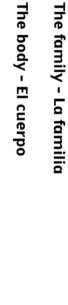

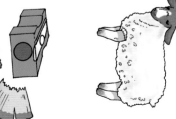

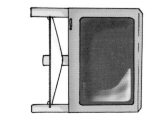

About this book

This picture dictionary presents familiar scenes and objects in a child's world. On each page, there are pictures labeled in Spanish so that the child can practice saying the words. At the back of the book is a word list listing the Spanish word, its pronunciation, and its English translation.

To help make learning fun, most pages double as an "I Spy" activity. Where is the newspaper in the family room picture? Where is the worm in the backyard picture? Children will enjoy looking for the objects that are pictured and named around the border of most pages.

Most of the words in this book are nouns (naming words). All Spanish nouns are masculine or feminine. You can tell if a word is masculine or feminine by the little word that comes before the noun. **El** is the word for "the" in front of a masculine noun and **la** is "the" in front of a feminine noun. For example, **el traspatio** means "the backyard" and **la casa** means "the house."

In front of nouns that are plural (more than one object, such as 'peas') use **los** if they are masculine and **las** if they are feminine. For example "peas" are **los guisantes** and "eyelashes" are **las pestañas.**

The family – La familia

brother
el hermano

father
el padre

mother
la madre

sister
la hermana

baby
el bebé

grandfather
el abuelo

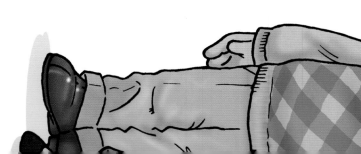

uncle **el tío**

aunt **la tía**

male cousin **el primo**

female cousin **la prima**

grandmother **la abuela**

The body
El cuerpo

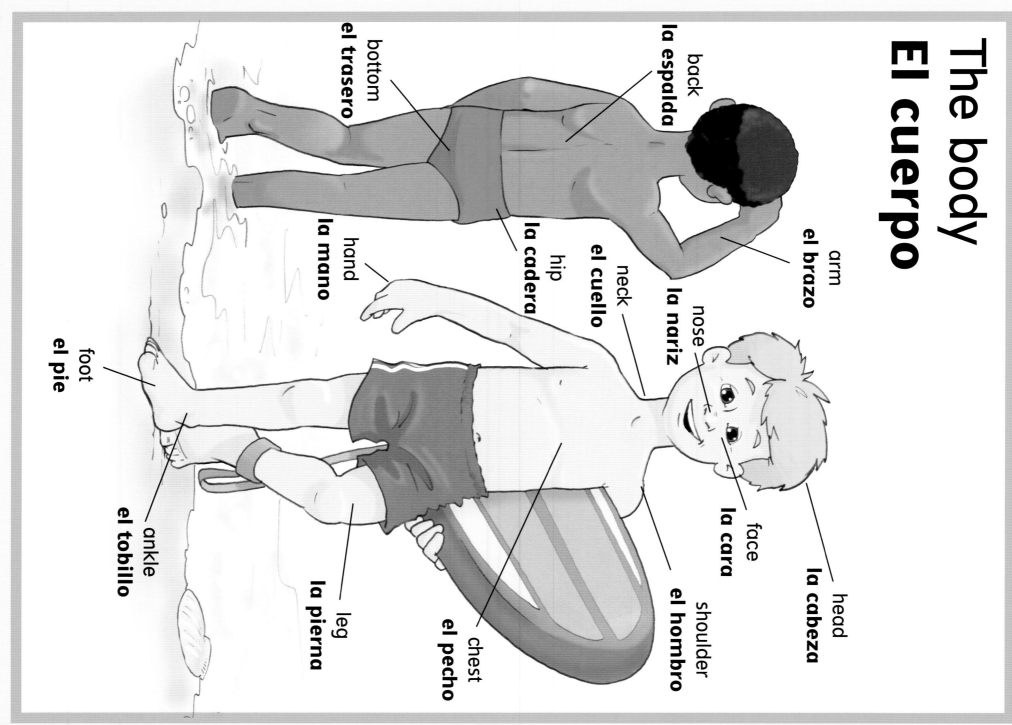

arm
el brazo

back
la espalda

bottom
el trasero

hand
la mano

hip
la cadera

neck
el cuello

nose
la nariz

face
la cara

head
la cabeza

shoulder
el hombro

chest
el pecho

leg
la pierna

ankle
el tobillo

foot
el pie

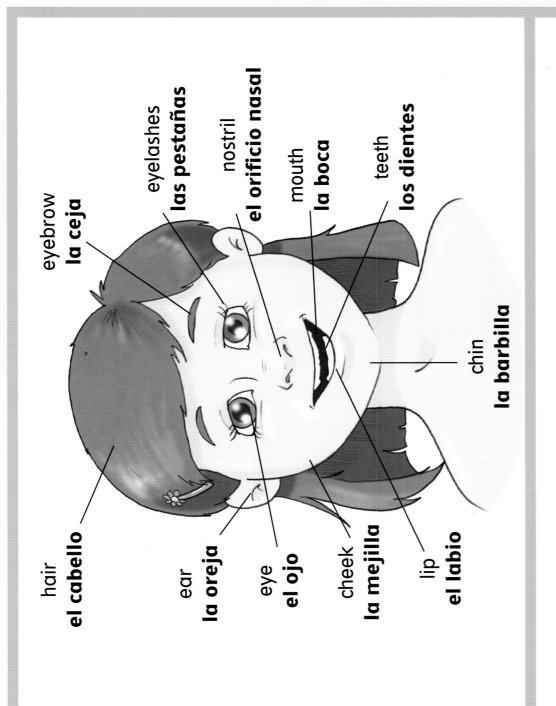

eyelashes
las pestañas

nostril
el orificio nasal

eyebrow
la ceja

mouth
la boca

teeth
los dientes

chin
la barbilla

hair
el cabello

ear
la oreja

eye
el ojo

cheek
la mejilla

lip
el labio

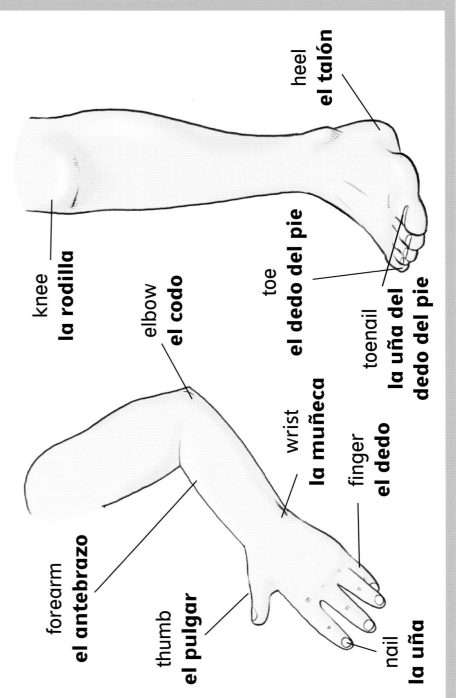

heel
el talón

knee
la rodilla

elbow
el codo

toe
el dedo del pie

toenail
la uña del dedo del pie

wrist
la muñeca

finger
el dedo

forearm
el antebrazo

thumb
el pulgar

nail
la uña

Colors – Los colores

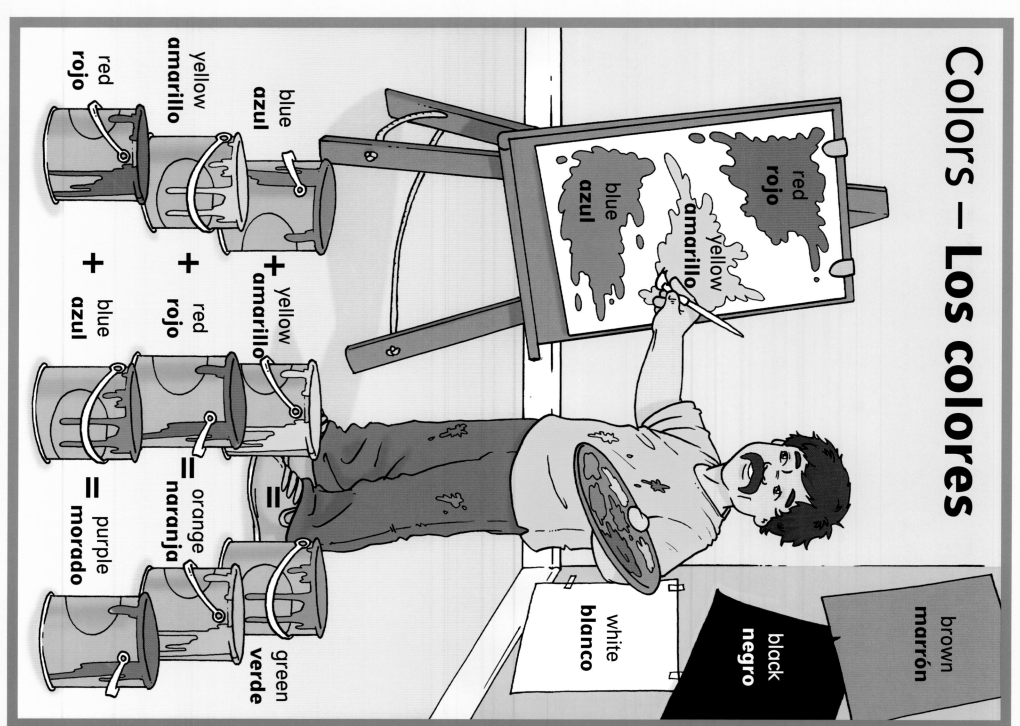

red
rojo

blue
azul

yellow
amarillo

red
rojo

blue
azul

yellow
amarillo

+

yellow
amarillo

+

red
rojo

+

blue
azul

=

orange
naranja

=

green
verde

=

purple
morado

white
blanco

black
negro

brown
marrón

Shapes – Las formas

rectangle
el rectángulo

crescent
la medialuna

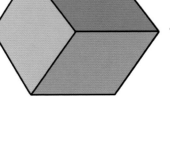

heart
el corazón

cube
el cubo

circle
el círculo

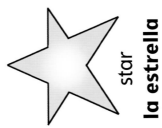

triangle
el triángulo

star
la estrella

cone
el cono

square
el cuadrado

diamond
el rombo

oval
el óvalo

cylinder
el cilindro

Numbers
Los números

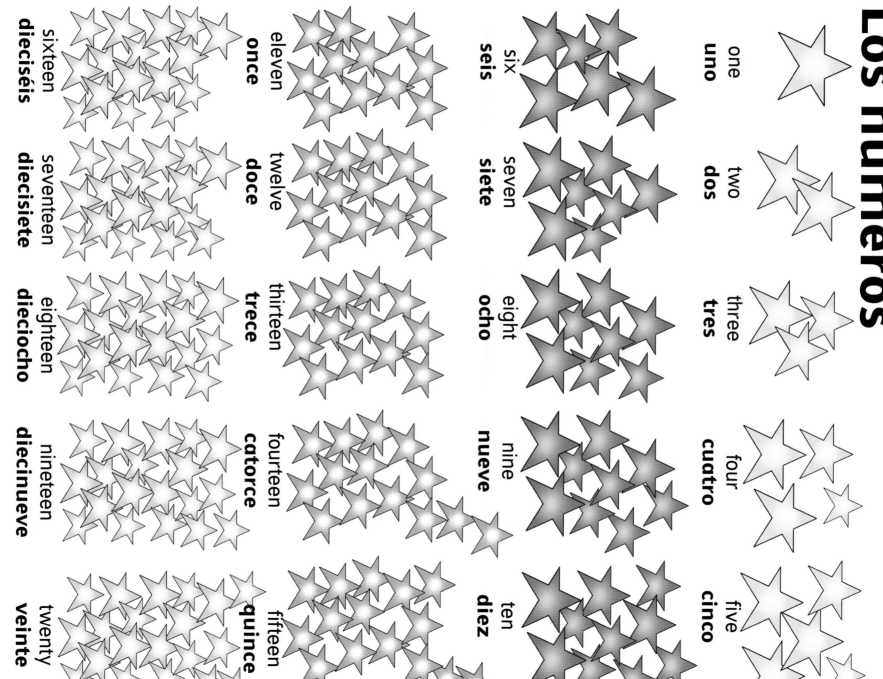

one
uno

two
dos

three
tres

four
cuatro

five
cinco

six
seis

seven
siete

eight
ocho

nine
nueve

ten
diez

eleven
once

twelve
doce

thirteen
trece

fourteen
catorce

fifteen
quince

sixteen
dieciséis

seventeen
diecisiete

eighteen
dieciocho

nineteen
diecinueve

twenty
veinte

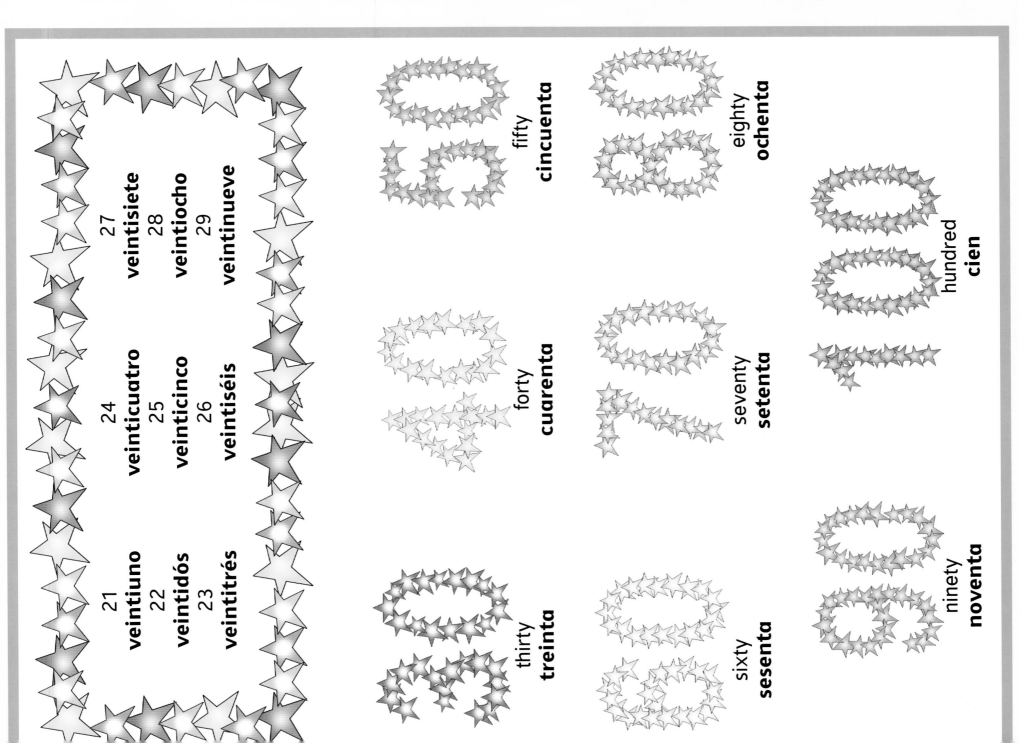

21 veintiuno
22 veintidós
23 veintitrés

24 veinticuatro
25 veinticinco
26 veintiséis

27 veintisiete
28 veintiocho
29 veintinueve

thirty
treinta

forty
cuarenta

fifty
cincuenta

sixty
sesenta

seventy
setenta

eighty
ochenta

ninety
noventa

hundred
cien

Mealtimes – Las horas de comer

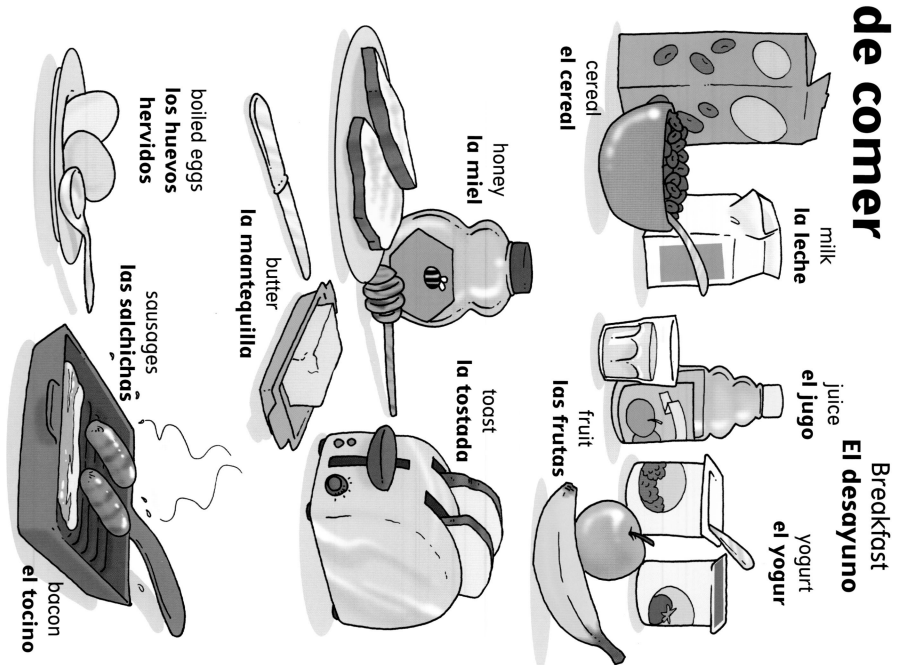

Breakfast
El desayuno

cereal
el cereal

milk
la leche

juice
el jugo

yogurt
el yogur

fruit
las frutas

honey
la miel

toast
la tostada

butter
la mantequilla

boiled eggs
**los huevos
hervidos**

sausages
las salchichas

bacon
el tocino

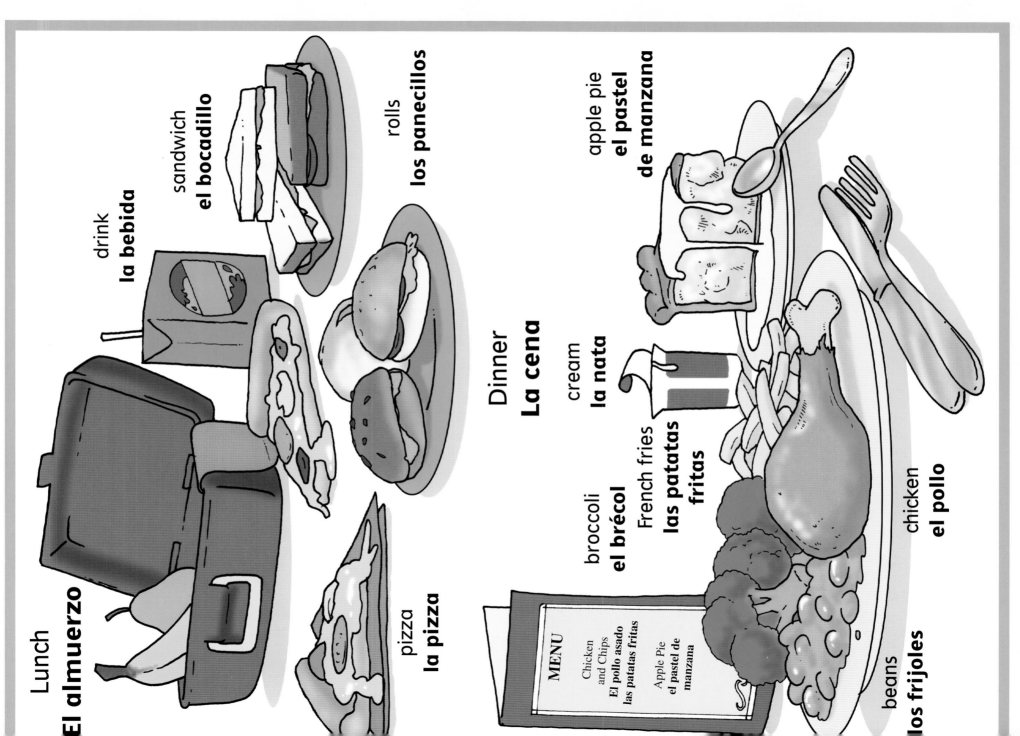

Lunch
El almuerzo

drink
la bebida

sandwich
el bocadillo

rolls
los panecillos

pizza
la pizza

Dinner
La cena

cream
la nata

broccoli
el brécol

French fries
las patatas fritas

apple pie
el pastel de manzana

chicken
el pollo

beans
los frijoles

MENU

Chicken
and Chips
**El pollo asado
las patatas fritas**

Apple Pie
**el pastel de
manzana**

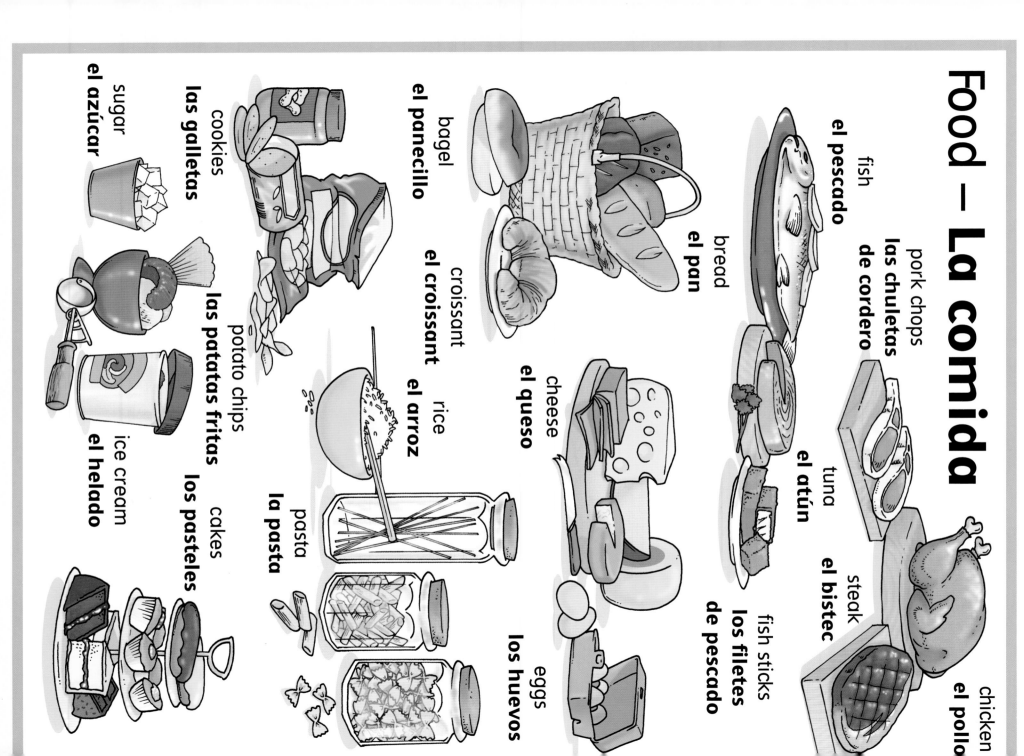

Food – La comida

fish
el pescado

pork chops
**las chuletas
de cordero**

bread
el pan

tuna
el atún

steak
el bistec

fish sticks
**los filetes
de pescado**

chicken
el pollo

bagel
el panecillo

croissant
el croissant

rice
el arroz

cheese
el queso

pasta
la pasta

eggs
los huevos

sugar
el azúcar

cookies
las galletas

potato chips
las patatas fritas

cakes
los pasteles

ice cream
el helado

Drink – La bebida

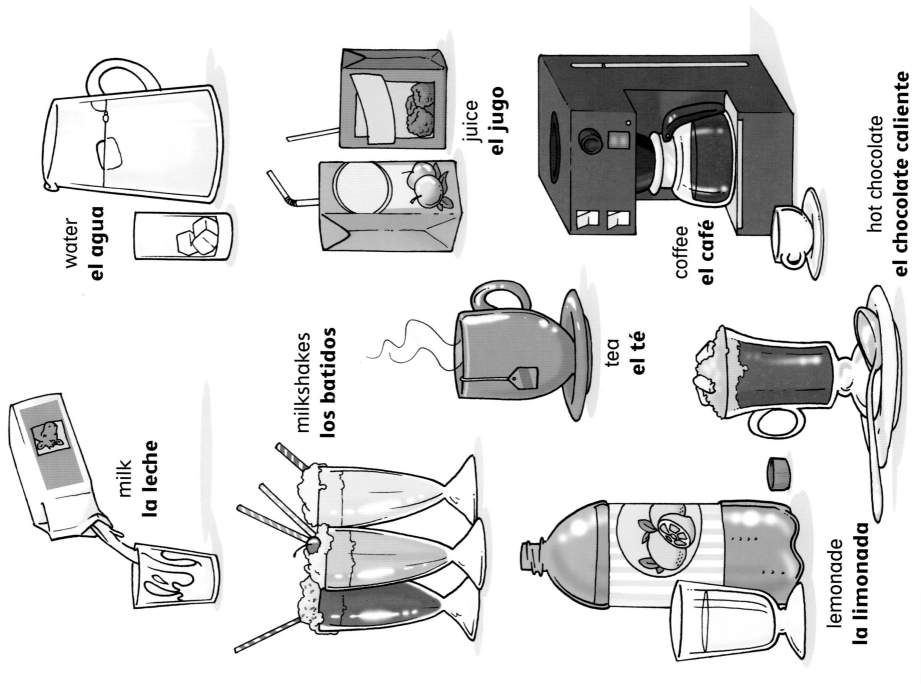

water **el agua**

juice **el jugo**

coffee **el café**

hot chocolate **el chocolate caliente**

milk **la leche**

milkshakes **los batidos**

tea **el té**

lemonade **la limonada**

Fruit – Las frutas

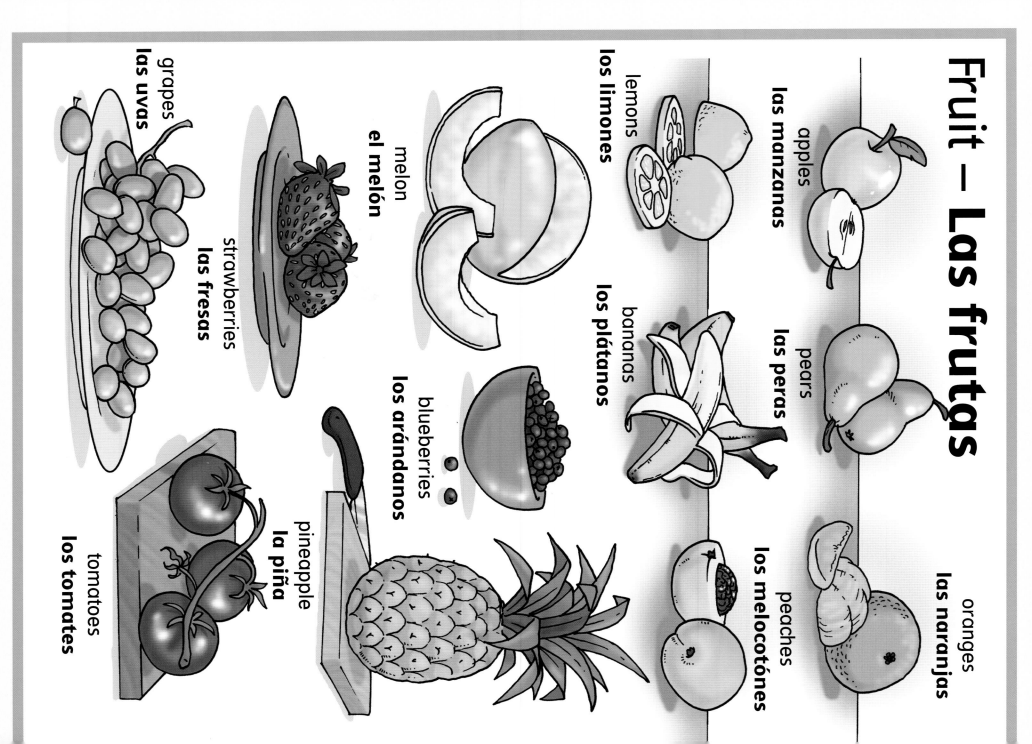

apples
las manzanas

pears
las peras

oranges
las naranjas

lemons
los limones

bananas
los plátanos

peaches
los melocotónes

melon
el melón

blueberries
los arándanos

grapes
las uvas

strawberries
las fresas

pineapple
la piña

tomatoes
los tomates

Vegetables – Las verduras

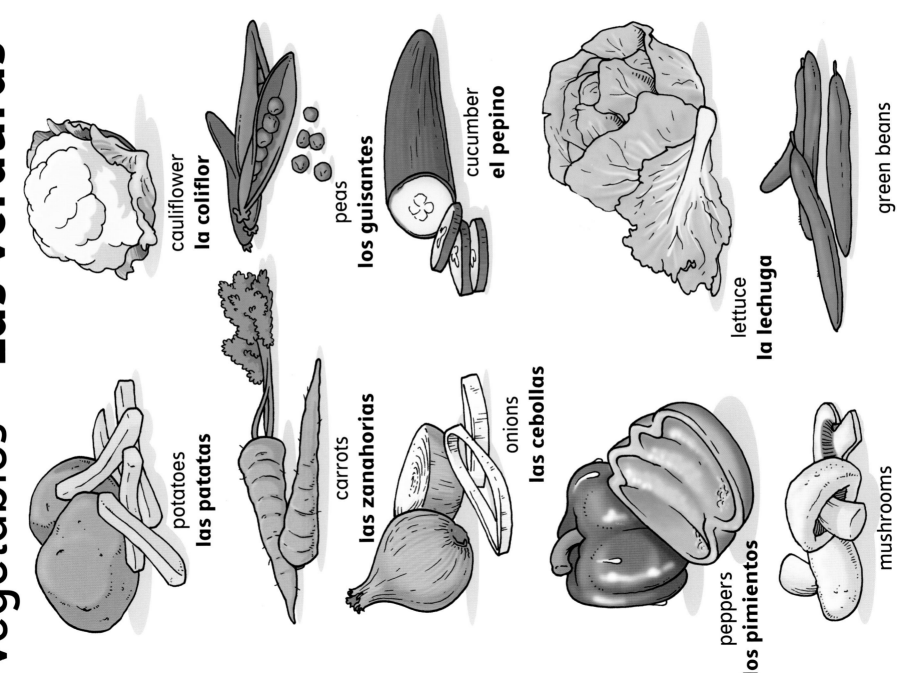

cauliflower
la coliflor

peas
los guisantes

cucumber
el pepino

green beans
las judías

lettuce
la lechuga

potatoes
las patatas

carrots
las zanahorias

onions
las cebollas

peppers
los pimientos

mushrooms
los champiñones

The Kitchen

apron
el delantal

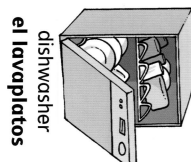

mixing bowl
el cuenco

clock
el reloj

wooden spoon
la cuchara de madera

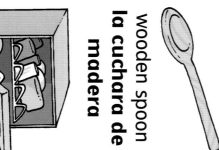

dishwasher
el lavaplatos

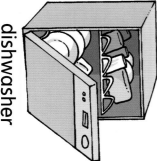

whisk
el batidor

butter
la mantequilla

kitchen knife
el cuchillo de cocina

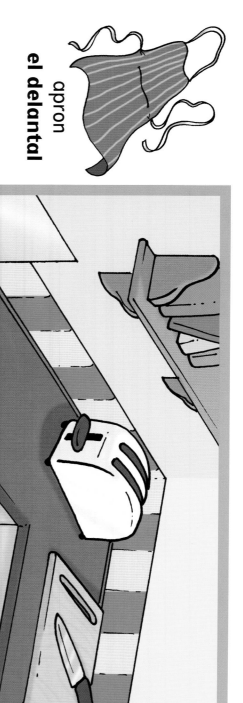

La cocina

sink
el fregadero

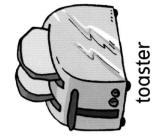
toaster
la tostadora

chair
la silla

microwave
la microonda

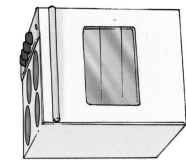
stove
la estufa

cutting board
el tajadero

can opener
el abrelatas

mug
el tazón

The table

pitcher
el jarro
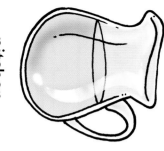

plate
el plato

casserole dish
la cazuela

soup spoon
**la cuchara
de sopa**

soup bowl
el tazón de sopa
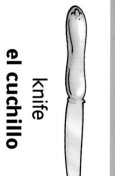

knife
el cuchillo

butter dish
la mantequera

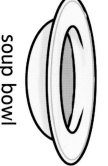

La mesa

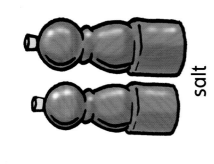

salt
la sal
pepper
la pimienta

napkin
la servilleta

teaspoon
la cucharilla

cup and saucer
**la taza
y el platillo**

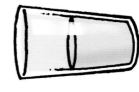

glass
el vaso

side plate
el platillo

fork
el tenedor

spoon
la cuchara

The family room

stool
el taburete

plant
la planta

armchair
el sillón

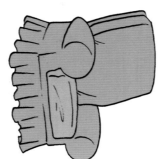

fireplace
la chimenea

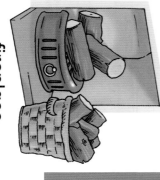

radio
la radio

newspaper
el periódico

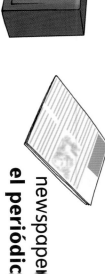

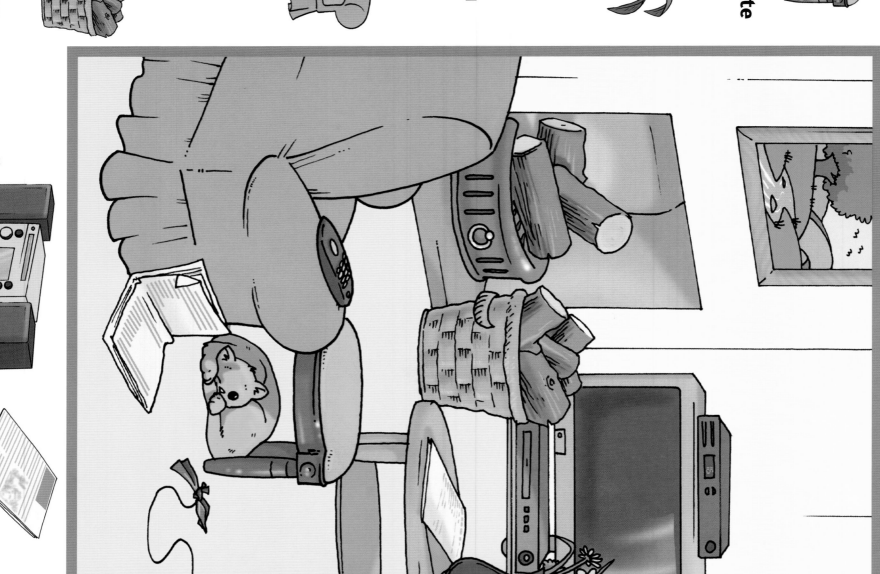

El cuarto de estar

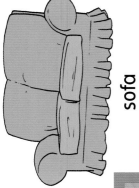

sofa
el sofá

vase
el florero

picture
el cuadro

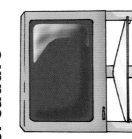

television
la televisión

window
la ventana

curtains
las cortinas

video player
el video

magazine
la revista

The bedroom

slippers
las zapatillas

baseball cap
la gorra de béisbol

socks
los calceties

running shoes
los zapatos de correr

chest of drawers
la cómoda

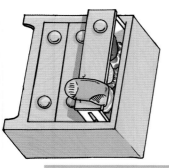

comb
el peine

brush
el cepillo

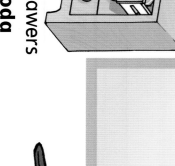

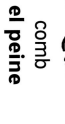

El dormitorio

t-shirt
la camiseta

jeans
los pantalones vaqueros

lamp
la lámpara

mirror
el espejo

teddy bear
el oso de peluche

bed
la cama

jigsaw puzzle
el rompecabezas

shoes
los zapatos

The bathroom

toilet
el inodoro

robe
la bata

sink
el lavabo

shelf
el estante

shower
la ducha

rubber duck
el pato de goma

soap
el jabón

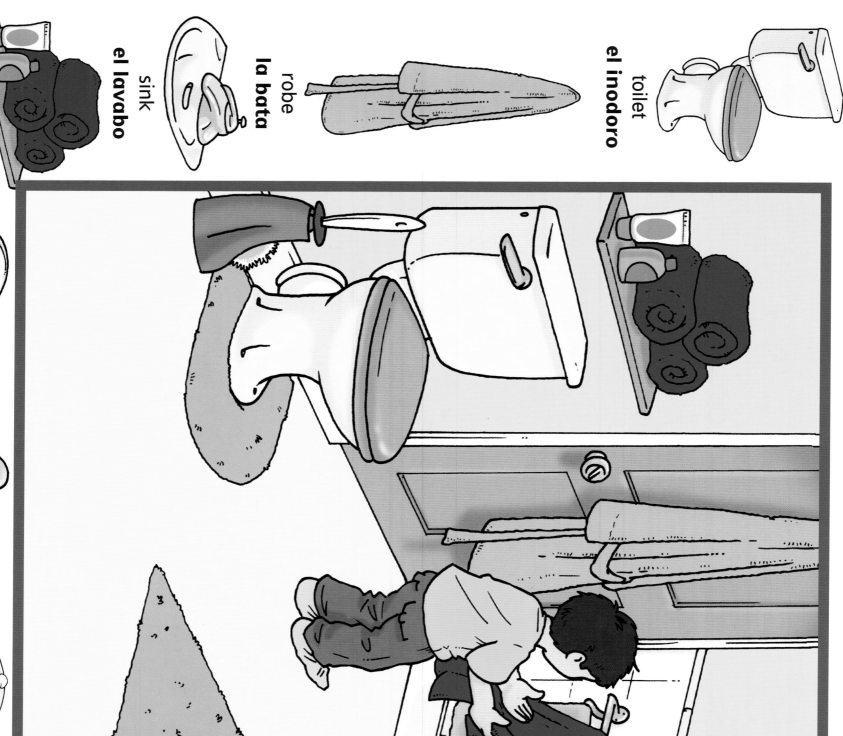

El cuarto de baño

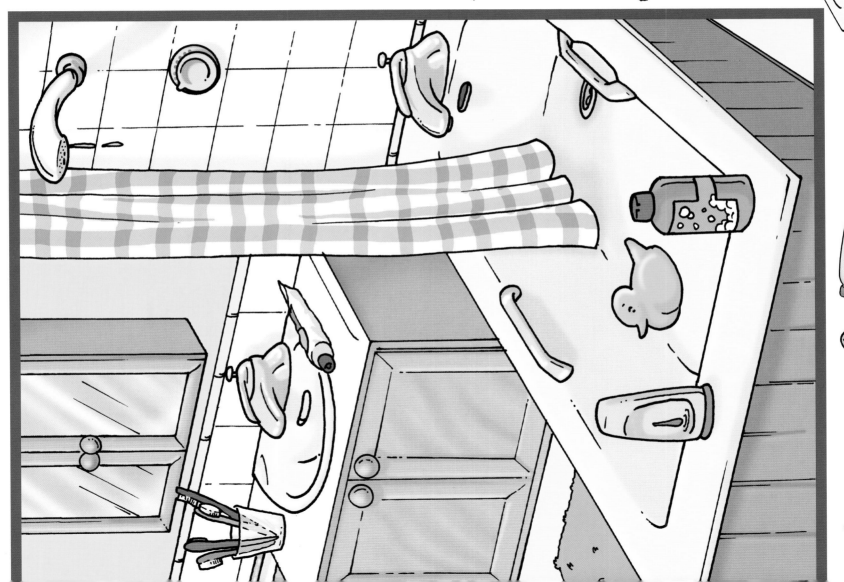

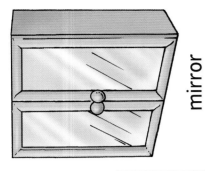
mirror
el espejo

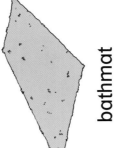
bubble bath
la espuma de baño

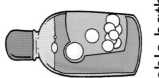
bathmat
la alfombrilla

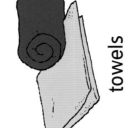
towels
las toallas

bathtub
la bañera

shampoo
el champú

towel rack
el toallero

The backyard

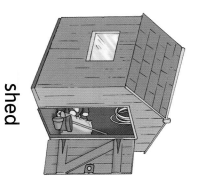

shed
el cobertizo

watering can
la regadera

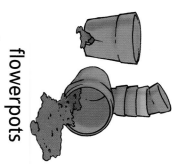

flowerpots
las macetas

tree
el árbol

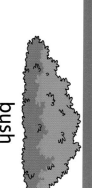

bush
el arbusto

snail
el caracol

El traspatio

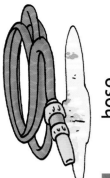

hose
la manguera

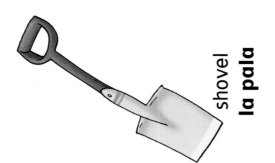

shovel
la pala

flowers
las flores

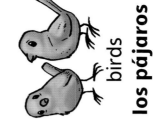

birds
los pájaros

wheelbarrow
la carretilla

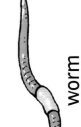

butterfly
la mariposa

worm
el gusano

Pets
Los animales domésticos

kittens
los gatitos

cat
el gato

dog
el perro

puppies
los cachorros

goldfish
el pez dorado

guinea pig
**el conejillo
de Indias**

hamster
el hámster

tortoise
la tortuga

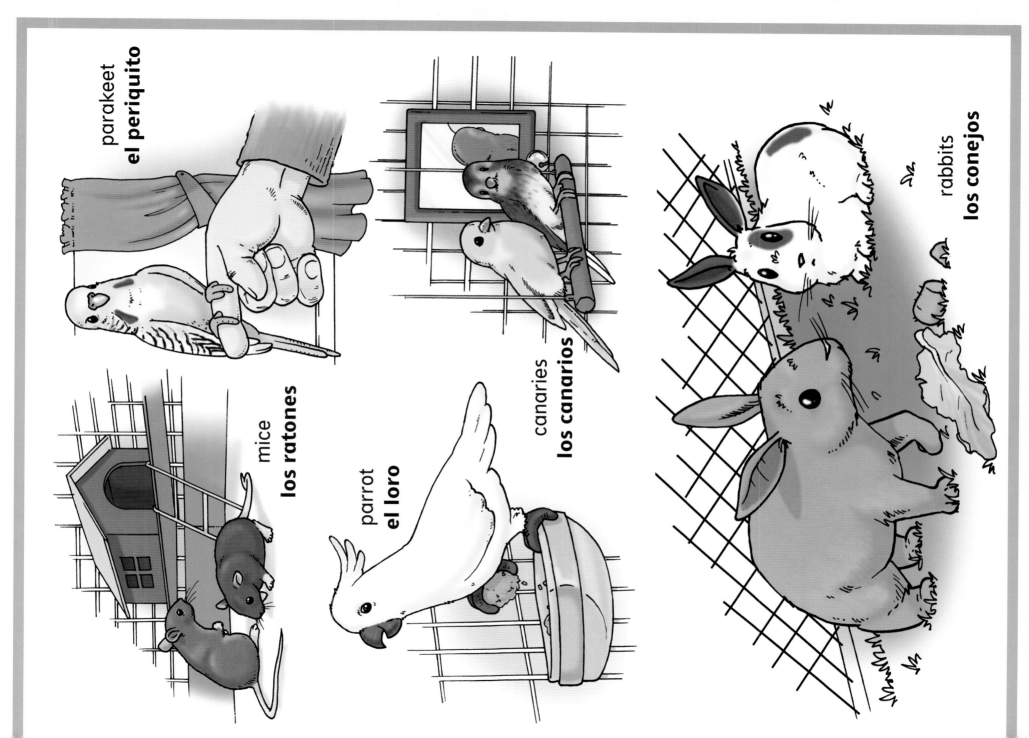

parakeet **el periquito**

canaries **los canarios**

rabbits **los conejos**

mice **los ratones**

parrot **el loro**

The farm

farmer
el granjero

cow
la vaca

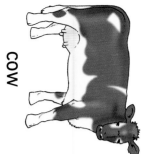

calf
el ternero

bull
el toro

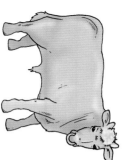

gate
la verja

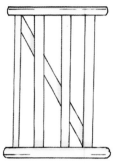

rooster
el gallo

chick
el pollito

La granja

tractor
el tractor

goat
la cabra

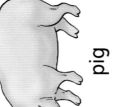
pig
el cerdo

sheep
la oveja

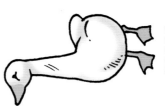
goose
el ganso

duck
el pato

hay
el heno

hen
la gallina

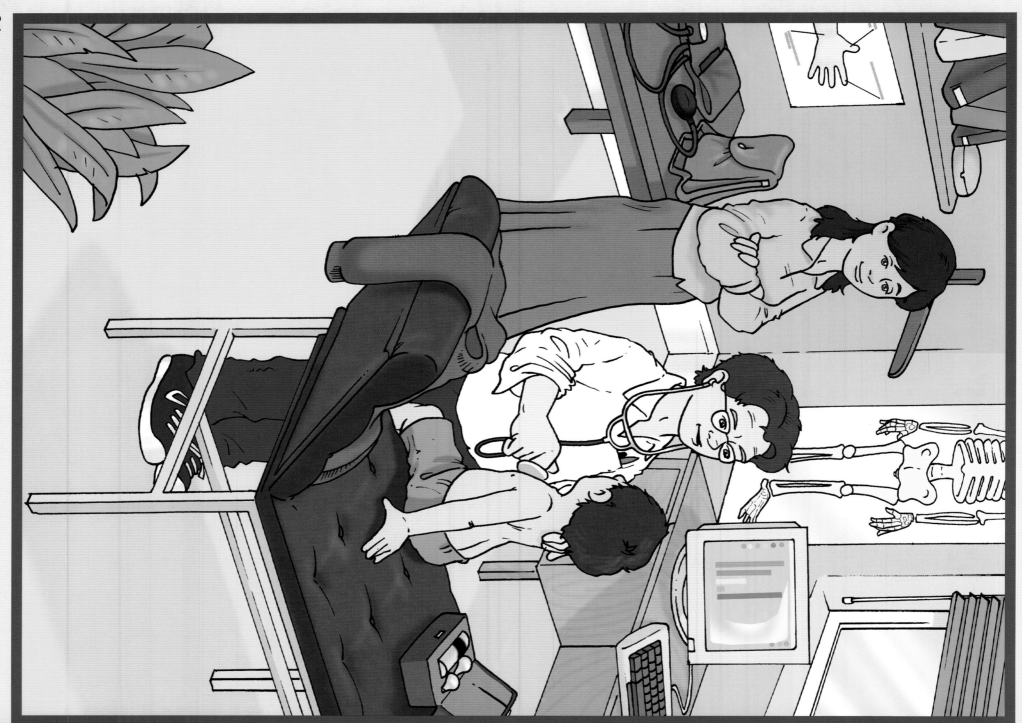

The doctor – El médico

bandages
las vendas

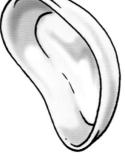
gauze
la gaza

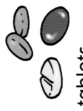

tablets
las pastillas

instrument dish
el plato de instrumentos

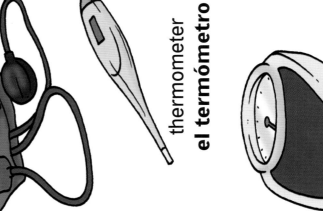
medicine bottle
la botella de la medicina

scissors
las tijeras

medical book
el libro médico

thermometer
el termómetro

scale
la báscula

stethoscope
el estetoscopio

syringe
la jeringuilla

blood pressure cuff
el instrumento de tomar la presión sanguínea

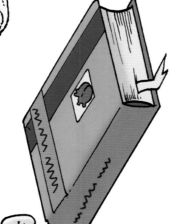
height gauge
el indicador de la estatura

The dentist – El dentista

dentist
el dentista

dental hygienist
la higienista dental

tissues
los pañuelos de papel

mouthwash
el enjuague

false teeth
las dentaduras postizas

sink
el lavabo

dentist's chair
la silla del dentista

toothbrush
el cepillo de dientes

toothpaste
la pasta dentífrica

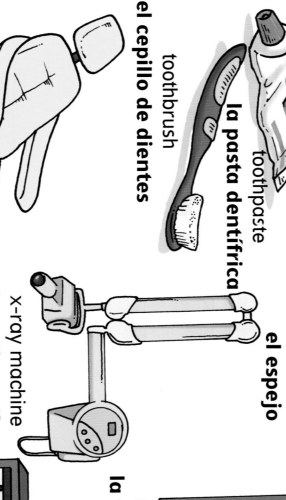

dental mirror
el espejo

x-ray machine
la radiografía

record chart
la tabla médica

light box
la caja de luz

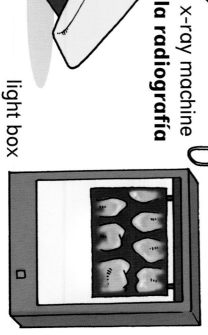

The classroom

teacher
la maestra

paper
el papel

globe
el globo

textbook
el libro de texto

backpack
la cartera

pencils
los lápices

ruler
la regla

pencil sharpener
el sacapuntas

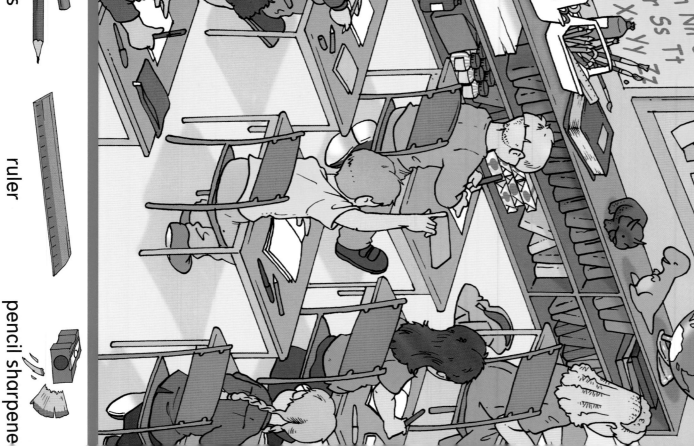

El salón de clases

computer
la computadora

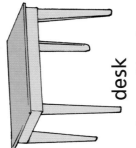

desk
el escritorio

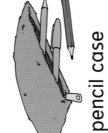

glue
la cola

pencil case
el estuche

crayons
**los lápices
de cera**

paints
las pinturas

eraser
la goma de borrar

paintbrushes
los pinceles

scissors
las tijeras

Sports
Los deportes

swimming
la natación

soccer
el fútbol

basketball
el baloncesto

ice skating
el patinaje

horse riding
la equitación

gymnastics
la gimnasia

running
el correr

baseball
el béisbol

snowboarding **el snowboarding**

skiing **el esquí**

football **el fútbol norteamericano**

cycling **el ciclismo**

judo **el judo**

tennis **el tenis**

golf **el golf**

Word list

This is a list of all the Spanish words in this book, arranged in alphabetical order, followed b[y] the word in English.

Tips for saying the words correctly. The following are some letters that are pronounced differen[t] in Spanish. Here's how to say them:

j as in the "**ch**" in the English word "**loch**"

ll as in "**I**" and "**y**" together, as in the "**ll**" in "**million**"

ñ as in the "**n**" in "**onion**"

qu as in the "**k**" in "**kite**"

r as in a rolled "**rrrr**"

v as in "**b**" in "**bat**"

z as in "**th**" in "**think**"

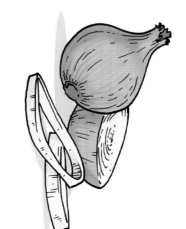

A

Spanish	Pronunciation	English
el abrelatas	el abraylAtas	can opener
la abuela	la aBWEla	grandmother
el abuelo	el aBWElo	grandfather
el agua	agwa	water
la alfombrilla	la alfombRREEya	bathmat
el almuerzo	el alMWERtho	lunch
amarillo	amaREELyo	yellow
los animales domésticos	loss aneeMAIess doMESSteekoss	pets
el antebrazo	el anteeBRAtho	forearm
los arándanos	los aRANdanos	blueberries
el árbol	el ARbol	tree
el arbusto	el arBOOSSto	bush
el arroz	el arroth	rice
el atún	el aTOON	tuna
el azúcar	el aTHOOkar	sugar
azul	aTHOOL	blue

B

Spanish	Pronunciation	English
el baloncesto	el balonSESto	basketball
la bañera	la banYAIRa	bathtub
la barbilla	la barBEELya	chin
la báscula	la BASkoola	scale
la bata	la BAta	robe
el batidor	el bateeDOR	whisk
los batidos	los baTEEdos	milkshakes
el bebé	el bayBAY	baby
la bebida	la bayBEEda	drink
el béisbol	el BAYSbol	baseball
el bistec	el BEEstek	steak
blanco	BLANko	white
la boca	la BOka	mouth
el bocadillo	el bokaDEELyo	sandwich
la botella de medicina	la boTELya day medeeSEEna	medicine bottle
el brazo	el BRAtho	arm
el brécol	el BRAYkol	broccoli

C

Spanish	Pronunciation	English
el cabello	el kaBELyo	hair
la cabeza	la kaBETHa	head
la cabra	la KAbra	goat
los cachorros	los kaCHOrross	puppies
la cadera	la kaDAYra	hip
el café	el kaFAY	coffee
la caja de luz	la kaha day LOOTH	light box
los calcenties	los kaltheTEEness	socks
la cama	la KAma	bed
la camiseta	la kamiSEta	t-shirt
los canarios	los kaNAReeoss	canaries
la cara	la KAra	face
el caracol	el karaKOL	snail
la carretilla	la karreTEELya	wheelbarrow
la cartera	la karTAIRa	backpack
catorce	kaTORthay	fourteen
la cazuela	la kaTHWELa	casserole dish
las cebollas	las thayBOLyas	onions
la ceja	la THAYha	eyebrow
la cena	la THAYna	dinner
el cepillo	el thePEELyo	brush
el cepillo de dientes	el thePEELyo day dee-ENtess	toothbrush
el cerdo	el THAIRdo	pig
el cereal	el tharayAL	cereal
el ciclismo	el theeKLEEZmo	cycling
cien	THEE-en	hundred
el cilindro	el theeLEENdro	cylinder
cinco	THINko	five
cincuenta	thinKWENta	fifty
el círculo	el THEERkoolo	circle
el cobertizo	el kobairTEEtho	shed
la cocina	la koSEENa	kitchen
el codo	el KOdo	elbow
la cola	la KOla	glue
la coliflor	la koleeFLOR	cauliflower
los colores	los koLORes	colors
la comida	la koMEEda	food
la cómoda	la KOmoda	chest of drawers
la computadora	la komPOOtadOra	computer
el conejillo de Indias	el kone-HEELyo day EENdeeyass	guinea pig
los conejos	los koNAYhoss	rabbits
el cono	el KOno	cone
el corazón	el koraTHON	heart
el correr	el koRAIr	running
las cortinas	las korTEEnas	curtains
el croissant	el KROYsan	croissant
el cuadrado	el kwaDRAdo	square
el cuadro	el KWAdro	picture
cuarenta	kwaRENTa	forty
el cuarto de baño	el KWARto day BANyo	bathroom
el cuarto de estar	el KWARto day essTAR	family room
cuatro	KWAtro	four
el cubo	el KOObo	cube
la cuchara	la kooCHAra	spoon
la cuchara de madera	la kooCHAra day maDAIRa	wooden spoon
la cuchara de sopa	la kooCHAra day SOpa	soup spoon
la cucharilla	la koochaREELya	teaspoon

Spanish	Pronunciation	English
el cuchillo	el kooCHEELyo	knife
el cuchillo de cocina	el kooCHEELyo day koSEEna	kitchen knife
el cuello	el KWELyo	neck
el cuenco	el KWENko	mixing bowl
el cuerpo	el KWAIRpo	body
CH		
los champiñones	los champeenYONess	mushroom
el champú	el champOO	shampoo
la chimenea	la cheemeNAYa	fireplace
el chocolate caliente	el chokolAtay kalee-ENtay	hot chocolate
las chuletas de cordero	lass chooLEtas day korDAIRo	pork chops
D		
el dedo	el DEdo	finger
el dedo del pie	el DEdo del pee-AY	toe
el delantal	el daylanTAL	apron
las dentaduras postizas	las dentaDOORass poseeTEEZass	false teeth
el dentista	el denTEESSta	dentist
los deportes	los dayPORtess	sports
el desayuno	el desSAIYuno	breakfast
dieciocho	dee-etheeOcho	eighteen
diecinueve	dee-etheeNWEbay	nineteen
dieciséis	dee-etheeSAYSS	sixteen
diecisiete	dee-etheeseeEtay	seventeen
los dientes	los dee-ENtess	teeth
diez	dee-ETH	ten
doce	DOthay	twelve
el dormitorio	el dormeeTORee-o	bedroom
dos	DOSS	two
la ducha	la DUcha	shower
E		
el enjuague	el enHWARgway	mouthwash
la equitación	la ekeetathee-ON	horse riding
el escritorio	el esskreeTORRee-o	desk
la espalda	la essPALda	back
el espejo	el essPAYho	mirror
la espuma de baño	la essPOOMa day BANyo	bubble bath
el esquí	el essKEE	skiing
el estante	el essTANtay	shelf
el estetoscopio	el esstetoSKOPee-o	stethoscope
la estrella	la essTRELya	star
el estuche	el essTOOchay	pencil case
la estufa	la essTOOfa	stove
F		
la familia	la faMEELya	family
los filetes de pescado	los feeLAYtess day pesKAdo	fish sticks
el florero	el floRAIRo	vase
las flores	las FLOrayss	flowers
las formas	las FORMas	shapes
el fregadero	el fregaDAYro	sink (kitchen)
las fresas	las FREssass	strawberries
los frijoles	los freeHOles	beans
las frutas	lass FROOtass	fruit
el fútbol	el FOOTbol	soccer
el fútbol norteamericano	el FOOTbol NORtayamayreekANo	football
G		
las galletas	lass galYETass	cookies
la gallina	la galYEENa	hen

Spanish	Pronunciation	English
el gallo	el gAIYo	rooster
el ganso	el GANzo	goose
los gatitos	los gaTEEtoss	kittens
el gato	el GAto	cat
la gaza	la gaSSa	gauze
la gimnasia	la heemNASSee-a	gymnastics
el globo	el GLObo	globe
el golf	el GOLF	golf
la goma de borrar	la GOma day borrar	eraser
la gorra de béisbol	la gooRa day BaissBoll	baseball cap
la granja	la GRANha	farm
el granjero	el granHAIRo	farmer
los guisantes	loss geeSSANtess	peas
el gusano	el gooSSAno	worm

H

Spanish	Pronunciation	English
el hámster	el AMstair	hamster
el helado	el ayLAdo	ice cream
el heno	el Eno	hay
la hermana	la airMANa	sister
el hermano	el airMANo	brother
la higienista dental	la EEhe-enEEsta denTAL	dental hygienist
el hombro	el OMbro	shoulder
las horas de comer	lass Oras day Komair	mealtimes
los huevos	los WEboss	eggs
los huevos hervidos	los WEboss erVIdoss	boiled eggs

I

Spanish	Pronunciation	English
el indicador de la estatura	el eendikaDOR day la esstaTOORa	height gauge
el inodoro	el inoDORo	toilet
el instrumento de tomar la presión sanguínea	el eenstrooMENto day toMAR la pretheeON sangweeNAY-ya	blood pressure cuff

J

Spanish	Pronunciation	English
el jabón	el haBON	soap
el jarro	el Harro	pitcher
la jeringuilla	la hereenGEELya	syringe
las judías	lass HOOdeeass	green beans
el judo	el JOOdo	judo
el jugo	el HOOgo	juice

L

Spanish	Pronunciation	English
el labio	el LAbee-o	lip
la lámpara	la LAMpara	lamp
los lápices	los LApeethess	pencils
los lápices de cera	loss laPEEthess day THAYra	crayons
el lavabo	el LAbabo	sink
el lavaplatos	el labaPLAtos	dishwasher
la leche	la LAYchay	milk
la lechuga	la layCHOOga	lettuce
el libro de texto	el LEEbro day TEXto	textbook
el libro médico	el LEEbro MEdi-ko	medical book
la limonada	la leemonAda	lemonade
los limones	los leeMONess	lemons
el loro	el LOro	parrot

M

Spanish	Pronunciation	English
las macetas	las maSETass	flowerpots
la madre	la MAdray	mother
la maestra	la MYstra	teacher
la manguera	la manGAIRa	hose
la mano	la MAno	hand

Español	Pronunciación	English
la mantequilla	la mantayKEEya	butter
la mantequera	la mantayKAIRa	butter dish
las manzanas	las manTHAnass	apples
la mariposa	la mareePOSSa	butterfly
marrón	maRRON	brown
la medialuna	la MEdee-aLOOna	crescent
el médico	el MEdeeko	doctor
la mejilla	la meHEELya	cheek
el melón	el meLON	melon
los melocotónes	los melekoTOMNess	peaches
la mesa	la MEssa	table
la microonda	la mickroOnda	microwave
la miel	la mee-EL	honey
morado	morAdo	purple
la muñeca	la mooNYEKa	wrist
N		
naranja	naRANha	orange
las naranjas	las naRANhass	oranges
la nariz	la naREETH	nose
la nata	la NAta	cream
la natación	la natathee-ON	swimming
negro	NEgro	black
noventa	noBENta	ninety
nueve	NWEbay	nine
los números	los NOOmeros	numbers
O		
ochenta	oCHENta	eighty
ocho	Ocho	eight
el ojo	el Oho	eye
once	ONthay	eleven
la oreja	la oREha	ear
el orificio nasal	el oreeFEESeo naZAL	nostril
el oso de peluche	el Osso day peLOOchay	teddy bear
el óvalo	el Obalo	oval
la oveja	la oBEha	sheep
P		
el padre	el PADray	father
los pájaros	los PAhaross	birds
la pala	la PAla	shovel
el pan	el PAN	bread
el panecillo	el paneTHEEyo	bagel
los panecillos	los paneTHEEyoss	rolls
los pantalones vaqueros	los pantalOnes BaKAIRoss	jeans
los pañuelos de papel	loss panWELos day paPEL	tissues
el papel	el paPEL	paper
la pasta	la PASSta	pasta
la pasta	la PASSta	pasta
la pasta dentífrica	la PASSta denTREEfeeka	toothpaste
el pastel de manzana	el passTEL day manTHAna	apple pie
los pasteles	los passTELess	cakes
las pastillas	las passTEELyass	tablets
las patatas	lass paTAtass	potatoes
las patatas	lass paTAtass	potatoes
las patatas fritas	lass paTAtass FREEtas	potato chips
las patatas fritas	lass paTAtass FREEtas	French fries
el patinaje	el pateeNAhay	ice-skating
el pato	el PAto	duck
el pato de goma	el PAto day GOma	rubber duck
el pecho	el PEcho	chest
el peine	el PAYnay	comb

Spanish	Pronunciation	English
el pepino	el pePEEno	cucumber
las peras	las PEras	pears
el periódico	el peree-Odeeko	newspaper
el periquito	el pereeKEEto	parakeet
el perro	el PErro	dog
el pescado	el peskAdo	fish
las pestañas	lass pessTANyas	eyelashes
el pez dorado	el PETH doRAdo	goldfish
el pie	el pee-AY	foot
la pierna	la pee-AIRna	leg
la pimienta	la peemee-ENta	pepper
los pimientos	los peemee-ENtoss	peppers
la piña	la PEENya	pineapple
los pinceles	los peenTHELess	paintbrushes
las pinturas	lass peenTOORass	paints
la pizza	la PEETza	pizza
la planta	la PLANta	plant
los plátanos	los PLAtan-oss	bananas
el platillo	el plaTEELyo	side plate
el plato	el PLAto	plate
el plato de instrumentos	el PLAto day instrooMENtos	instrument dish
el pollito	el poLYEEto	chick
el pollo	el POLyo	chicken
la prima	la PREEma	female cousin
el primo	el PREEmo	male cousin
el pulgar	el pulGAR	thumb

Q

Spanish	Pronunciation	English
el queso	el KEsso	cheese
quince	KEENthay	fifteen

R

Spanish	Pronunciation	English
la radio	la RAdee-o	radio
la radiografía	la radee-o-graFEE-a	x-ray machine
los ratones	los raTONess	mice
el rectángulo	el rekTANgoolo	rectangle
la regadera	la regaDAIRa	watering can
la regla	la REgla	ruler
el reloj	el reLOH	clock
la revista	la reBEEsta	magazine
la rodilla	la roDEELya	knee
rojo	ROho	red
el rombo	el ROMbo	diamond
el rompecabezas	el rompaykaBEthas	jigsaw puzzle

S

Spanish	Pronunciation	English
el sacapuntas	el sakaPOONtas	pencil sharpener
la sal	la SAL	salt
las salchichas	las salCHEEchas	sausages
el salón de clases	el saalOn day cla-says	classroom
seis	SAYSS	six
la servilleta	la serveelYETa	napkin
sesenta	seSENta	sixty
setenta	seTENta	seventy
siete	see-Etay	seven
la silla	la SEELya	chair
la silla del dentista	la SEELya del denTEESSta	dentist's chair
el sillón	el seelYON	armchair
el snowboarding	el eSNOWbordeeng	snowboarding
el sofá	el soFA	sofa

Spanish	Pronunciation	English
T		
la tabla médica	la TAbla MEdica	record chart
el taburete	el tabooRETay	stool
el tajadero	el tahaDAIRo	cutting board
el talón	el taLON	heel
la taza y el platillo	la TAssa E el platEElyo	cup and saucer
el tazón	el taTHON	mug
el tazón de sopa	el taTHON day SOpa	soup bowl
el té	el TAY	tea
la televisión	la telebeessee-ON	television
el tenedor	el teneDOR	fork
el tenis	el TEneess	tennis
el termómetro	el tairMOmetro	thermometer
el ternero	el tairNAIRo	calf
la tía	la TEE-a	aunt
las tijeras	lass teeHAIRass	scissors
el tío	el TEE-o	uncle
las toallas	las to-ALyass	towels
el toallero	el to-alYAIRo	towel rack
el tobillo	el toBEELyo	ankle
el tocino	el toSEEno	bacon
los tomates	los toMAtayss	tomatoes
el toro	el TOro	bull
la tortuga	la torTOOga	tortoise
la tostada	la tossTAda	toast
la tostadora	la tosstaDORa	toaster
el tractor	el trakTOR	tractor
el trasero	el traSAIRo	bottom
el traspatio	el trassPATio	backyard
trece	TREthay	thirteen
treinta	treINta	thirty
tres	TRESS	three
el triángulo	el tree-ANgoolo	triangle
U		
la uña	la OOnya	nail
la uña del dedo del pie	la OOnya del dedo del peeAY	toenail
uno	OOno	one
las uvas	lass OObass	grapes
V		
la vaca	la BAka	cow
el vaso	el BAsso	glass
veinte	BAYntay	twenty
las vendas	lass BENdas	bandages
la ventana	la benTAna	window
verde	BAIRday	green
las verduras	lass bairDOORas	vegetables
la verja	la BAIRha	gate
el vídeo	el VIDayo	video player
Y		
el yogur	el yoGOOR	yogurt
Z		
las zanahorias	las thana-ORee-ass	carrots
las zapatillas	lass thapaTEELyas	slippers
los zapatos	los thaPAtoss	shoes
los zapatos de correr	los thaPAtoss day koRAIR	running shoes